THE

POWER

TO DECLARE

WAR

BY KAREN GATES

The Power To Declare War
Written By Karen Gates

For speaking engagements or request to reproduce this publication, contact the author at povministries@gmail.com or povministries.wordpress.com

Cover Graphic made with Canva

ISBN: 9798329412000

TABLE OF CONTENTS

INTRODUCTION

Matthew 16:18, Jesus says "You are Peter (petros) and on this rock (petra) I will build my church and the gates of hell shall not prevail against it. The church that is built upon the foundation of Jesus Christ, will advance forward regardless to the attacks of the kingdom of darkness. What the enemy tries to hurl at you to stop you from moving forward in your purpose,will not prevail (that means it will not accomplish that which it sets out to do). The power that is within you is more powerful than the power of this world.

I want you to know that you have the power within you to declare war against any enemy that comes to fight your faith, your purpose and your family. These fights come to distract or delay you from your destiny. The power that is within you called "The Holy Spirit" which is the Spirit of Truth, not only plays defense he plays offense too. It's time to take the fight to the enemy and throw the first punch. Every morning that we hit the floor we should be ready and score for the Kingdom of God. The people of God have become accustomed to fighting after we have been hit. What we don't understand is that the first blow can take you out or incapacitate you and take you out. It's time to dismantle and disarm the enemy. It's time to declare war!

Just like there are several branches of the natural army so it is in the spirit. There is a reason for each branch of the army. Each one has a specific environment in which they specialize when it comes to war. We all have been given weapons of war. These weapons make us an unstoppable force against the kingdom of darkness. Our most powerful weapon is prayer. What makes prayer effective is the ammo. The word of God is your ammo. The word of God is quick, powerful and sharper than any two-edged sword. What are you declaring war with? We wrestle not against flesh and blood so our weapons are not carnal (man-made).

If you're going to declare war you have to make sure you have the right weapons and know how to effectively use those weapons in battle. You have to know your target 's weaknesses and strengths because your opponent has studied you well. Each chapter serves as a bullet of the word of God to come against and take out spirits that come to bring down the people of God and destroy the reputation of the church.

YOU HAVE THE POWER IT'S TIME TO DECLARE WAR!!!!

DECLARE

To Make Evident to make known formally, officially or explicitly. To make the order known publicly.

WAR

 A conflict carried on by force of arms, as between nations or between parties within a nation; warfare, as by land, sea, or air. A state or period of armed hostility or active military operations.

Job 22:28 (KJV)

Thou shalt also decree a thing, and it shall be established unto thee: and the light shall shine upon thy ways.

CHAPTER ONE

PROTECTION FOR THE FAMILY

CHAPTER ONE

PROTECTION FOR THE FAMILY

A family is a group of two or more persons related by birth, marriage, or adoption, who live together.

In Nehemiah chapter 4, Nehemiah positions the people with their families and their weapons and tells them not to fight each other and not to be fearful of the threats of the enemy, because God will fight for them.This is an awesome example of how families can come together putting aside any differences and stand together not just in times of trouble but times of building and celebration.

The sanctity of family shapes the character of who we are; family teaches us morals, traditions, how to love, how to unite and how to uplift each other in times of struggle. Family teaches us how to deal with life, death and trauma. It's bad enough that families have to deal with attacks in their natural lives but the added attacks fueled by unseen forces is added pressure. I am a firm believer that God calls families and certain people within a family to come against those spiritual attacks that come to break down the family unit and its purpose. The best way to deal with these attacks is to declare war!

PROTECTION FOR THE FAMILY

These scriptures will help you to strike blows in the spirit and bring down the kingdom of darkness.The plots and plans of the enemy are to infiltrate and tear down your family.

The bible says, Deuteronomy 31:6 (NIV) Be strong and courageous. Do not be afraid or terrified because of them, for the Lord your God goes with you; he will never leave you nor forsake you."

Ask God to place a hedge of protection around your family like he did for Job. The enemy does not want to see your family prosper, especially a God fearing family built on the foundation of Jesus Christ.

A God fearing family produces Godly fruit therefore increasing the Kingdom of God. Whatever the enemy can do to break down the family he will surely do.

God is calling you to rise up and cover your family. He has called you to be the watchman on the tower to sound the alarm. Fight for your family and the generations that will come After you.

PROTECTION FOR THE FAMILY

I declare Isaiah 54:17(NIV) that no weapon that is fashioned against my family shall succeed and my God will refute every tongue that rises against me in judgment.

I declare 2 Thessalonians 3:3 (NIV) that you Lord are faithful and you will establish me and my family and will guard us against the evil one. Lord I thank you for your word Psalm 46:1, which establishes that you are Our refuge and strength and a very present help in the time of trouble.

I declare that the love of God is a hedge around me and my family. This will allow us to live together In unity according to Psalm 133:1(NIV).

I declare that we don't have to fear because you are with us and we don't have to be dismayed for you are our God. You will strengthen us, and help us. You will uphold our family with your righteous right hand, Isaiah 41:10 (NIV). I declare that the Lord watches over the comings and goings of my family both now and forevermore to protect us according to Psalm 121:8 (NIV)

Karen Gates

The Power To Declare War

PROTECTION FOR THE FAMILY

I declare that you are a hiding place for us; you preserve us from trouble; you surround us with shouts of deliverance according to Psalms 32:7 (NIV).

We take up the shield of faith, that can extinguish all the fiery darts of the evil one according to Ephesians 6:16.

I declare our Lord is a shield about us, our glory, and the lifter of our head according to Psalm 3:3 (NIV).

I declare that the Lord is our rock and fortress and our deliverer, my God, my rock, in whom I take refuge, my shield and the horn of my salvation my stronghold according to Psalm 18:2 (NIV)

I declare that love does not delight in evil but rejoices with the truth. It always protects, always trusts, always hopes, always perseveres. 1 Corinthians 13:6. Lord, I thank you for being a good father and I ask for your protection for my family.

CHAPTER TWO

WAR FOR YOUR FAMILY

CHAPTER TWO

WAR FOR YOUR FAMILY

James 5:16 (KJV) The effectual fervent prayer of a righteous man availeth much. My question to you is are you righteous? In order to answer that you will need to know what the word means. Righteousness is living in a right relationship with God, other people, and all creation. Which also means that you're living according to God's instruction. This alone should give a person an indication regarding their prayers that aren't answered. God can hear everyone and their request but he wont move on everybody's request.

Whenever I need to gain understanding regarding a scripture I look up the meaning. It gives you a better understanding and perspective of how you see it and the way you should apply to your life.

So let's break down some of the words in this scripture, Availeth or avail mean to produce or result in as a benefit or advantage. A righteous prayer produces an advantage. Effectual is something that produces an intended effect or adequately fulfills its purpose. Fervent means passionate, constant or intense. So now look at this scripture with those definitions it is saying your righteous prayer when done passionately gives you the advantage to get the desired result you are seeking.

WAR FOR YOUR FAMILY

This should make all of us consider how we are living as a believer. We should be the one who our family sees walking out our salvation. Your prayer as a believer is the prayer that makes the difference. Your prayer for your family is their saving grace.

Have you ever had family members who mock you and laugh and say some not so nice things about you, because you choose to live and model your life after Christ.

But when they are in a situation they come to you for prayer. It's because they understand the way you live your life gets you favor with God in the prayer department.

I declare 1 Peter 4:8 9(NIV) That above all else we will love each other deeply. We should be covering and standing in the gap for our family daily. Say a special prayer for those who are caught in the vices of the world and tricks of the enemy that they just can't shake. It's our job to war against the powers and principalities of the kingdom of darkness that cannot be seen but has a tight grip on their life. I declare war on the spirit of unforgiveness within our family that comes to break down our unity with each other.

Colossians 3:13 (NLT) says we are to make allowances for each other and forgive one another if we have any type of grievances against someone we are to forgive as the Lord forgives us.

WAR FOR YOUR FAMILY

Show us how to forgive with our heart, body, mind and soul. I break down walls that separate us from each other. Let us find strength in you Lord that increases the unity in our family.

I break down every wall offense that has been built to block us from operating in patience and love with one another.

1 Corinthians 13:4-7(NIV) says, Love is patient, love is kind, love does not envy, it does not boast, it's not proud It does not dishonor, it's not self-seeking,it is not easily angered, it keeps no record of wrong because love covers a multitude of sins.

I declare war with gossip and backbiting within the family. We will not let any unwholesome talk come out of our mouths according to Ephesians 4:29 (NIV).

I declare war against the spirit of anger by utilizing Proverbs 15:1-4 (NIV).by giving gentle answers that will turn away wrath and not stir up anger. I declare we shall speak with a soothing tongue that is like a tree of life that will not crush a person's spirit. I declare love, peace and unity shall abide among us.

WAR FOR YOUR FAMILY

I declare war against generational curses by training up the children of the family in the way that they should go so that when they are old they will never turn away from it according to Proverbs 22:6 (NIV)

I declare that we shall spur one another on toward love and good deeds, not giving up meeting together as some are in the habit of doing,but encouraging one another according to Hebrews 10: 24-25 (NIV).

Lord I declare war on envy, pride, dishonor, anger, mistrust and replace them with love. Infuse your love throughout my bloodline from oldest to youngest. Let your love reign in our hearts and homes. Mend all of the broken places in my family. I declare that the captives are free, I come against addictions, curses and strife.

I declare that love casts out all fear that we may become united in one faith and belief that you are who you say you are and you will do what you said. I declare unity from generation to generation.

CHAPTER THREE

WAR ON POVERTY

CHAPTER THREE
WAR ON POVERTY

When we think of poverty our minds often go straight to lack of money which we interpret as finances. We do that because that is one aspect of poverty that we see in our everyday lives. Poverty has many faces and aspects of itself and it extends itself beyond a lack of finances. When I looked up the word poverty it is the state of being extremely poor, the state of being inferior in quality or insufficient amount.

The strong's concordance defines poverty as that which is lacking in need, things or persons which are lacking defects or shortcomings. That means in some way, we are all in poverty when we lack anything, it doesn't just have to be money. As I began to research more about poverty. I found that there are four types of poverty that top the list of what is defined as poverty.

Absolute poverty is when a person cannot meet the basic needs of living like food, water, and housing.

Relative poverty is when a person can meet the basic need but their income level is far below the average of the area they live in.

WAR ON POVERTY

Situational poverty is when circumstances of life like divorce, death,or serious illness impacts their finances.

Generational poverty is a poverty that lasts through many generations when children are born in poverty and they have children who are born in poverty and their children live in the same kind of poverty.

I believe these types of poverty are a direct result of a lack of knowledge,wisdom,understanding and training.

Growing up in some of the most poverty stricken areas in Chicago was like living in a bubble where you didn't really know anything outside the area where you lived, unless someone told you or your parents took you.
The biggest goal was getting out of the ghetto, getting out alive and making it big.

 When I got my first place as an adult which was a low income housing apartment. I felt I had accomplished this huge thing. Because I was now paying rent and bills on my own, I did not understand that I was still bound by the boundaries of where I lived. It was not until I left many years later that I began to realize that there was so much more beyond the state lines of Chicago.

WAR ON POVERTY

When I made the move out of state. I started to see that I could do things beyond just having a dream. I was one mindset away from coming out of what I thought was normal.

The more my mind was renewed the more knowledge I gained. That allowed not only me but my children to thrive. Now that we have Identified some of the most common forms of poverty, let's declare war on poverty.

I declare war on the spirit of poverty that would try to break down the prosperity of my bloodline. According to 2 Corinthians 9:6-7(NIV) states that the one who sows sparingly, and the one who sows bountifully will reap bountifully. I will give as I have made up in mind not giving reluctantly or under compulsion for God loves a cheerful giver.

I declare that I will open my hand to the poor and needy in the land according to Dueteronomy 15: 11(NIV).

I declare that if a brother or sister is naked and lacks daily food, I will not tell them to go in peace; keep warm, eat their fill, but I will supply their bodily needs as well according to James 2:15-17 (NIV).

WAR ON POVERTY

I declare war on poverty by showing kindness to the poor which is like lending to the Lord and he will reward me for what they have done according to Proverbs 19:17(AMP).

I declare that God will never forget the needy; and the hope of the afflicted will never perish according to Psalm 9:18 (NIV).

I declare war on poverty as he lifts the poor from the dust and the needy from the garbage dump.

I declare war on poverty by placing my hope in the Lord our God who made heaven and earth, the sea, and all that is in them; he who keeps faith forever; who executes justice for the oppressed; and he who gives food to the hungry according to Psalm 146:5-7.

I declare war on poverty by being anointed to preach bring the good news to the poor and proclaim freedom to the captives and recovery of sight to the blind, to let the oppressed go free, to proclaim the good news and the year of the Lord's favor according to Luke 4:18-19.

WAR ON POVERTY

I declare war on poverty according to Dueteronomy 15:10-11 (NIV) that says, since there will never cease to be some in need on the earth, I will open my hand to the poor and needy neighbor in my land.

I declare war on poverty by sharing my bread with the hungry, and bringing the homeless into my house and when I see the naked, I will cover them, and not hide myself from my own kin according to Isaiah 58:6-11 (NIV).

I declare that He shall set them among princes, placing them in seats of honor. For all the earth is the Lord's and he has set the world in order according to 1 Samuel 2:8 (NIV).

I declare war on poverty according to Job 5:15 (NIV) For God saves the needy from the sword in their mouth and from the clutches of their enemy

I declare because the Lord is a refuge and a stronghold for the oppressed, in times of trouble that poverty shall be broken over the lives of his people according to Psalm 9:9 (NIV). Blessed in the one who considers the poor,IMatthew 5:3 and 1 Timothy 6:18, Psalm 41:1.

WAR ON POVERTY

I declare war on poverty by speaking up for those who cannot speak for themselves; I will speak up for justice for those being crushed according to Proverbs 31:8 NIV).

I declare war on poverty by giving to the poor and not closing my eyes when I see a person living in poverty according to Proverbs 28:27(NIV).

I declare war on poverty by letting the words of my mouth and the meditation of my heart be acceptable in the sight of the Lord my rock and redeemer. Psalm 19:14 (NIV).

I declare war on poverty by keeping an open heart and a new mindset by not leaning to my own understanding as to why the poor are in the situation they are in according to Proverbs 3:5 (NIV)

God, I ask that you search me and I pray that my heart is found to be like yours, try my thoughts and see if there is a grievous way in me, lead me in the way of the everlasting according to Psalm 139:23-24 (NIV).

CHAPTER FOUR

WAR FOR YOUR MARRIAGE

CHAPTER FOUR

WAR FOR YOUR MARRIAGE

After God created man he instituted and established marriage. He looked upon his creation called man and said, "It is not good for man to be alone" so he created Eve for companionship and help. God didn't do a nuptial ceremony like we do today. In those days of the bible consummation (sex between the man and the woman is what sealed a marriage). Marriage was instituted for a reason and a purpose.

The purpose was for them to be fruitful, multiply and for mankind to subdue the earth. After God had given them their assignment within the earth their union was tested. So why do we think that our marriages and relationships won't be? The serpent used his cunning ways to divide, conquer, break down and take away mankind's God given authority.

The vows that are stated in a ceremony are a testament of how both parties will agree to live out their lives under the authority and rulership of God. It's about us coming together in one heart, one mind and one Spirit for the purpose of the Kingdom of Heaven.

WAR FOR YOUR MARRIAGE

The enemy does not want that couple to produce Godly fruit and a family that is built on the foundation of God.

I would tell my mentees that were having difficulties in their marriage that as long as both of you love God, seek God and commit to God by placing him in every aspect of your life and marriage there is nothing that is impossible for God to fix. It is in these times that you must fight the hardest for your union. You can overcome it by not allowing flesh and feelings to govern you to the point you're ready to walk away. But there are situations in which you should absolutely walk away. When the bible tells you be not unevenly yoked with an unbeliever, that is a different kind of fight and war that you have entered. It will either make you or break you. In the beginning of my marriage we were both in sin, living in sin and doing sin well. But I was now at a place In my life that I desired something different. Not only for me but for my children. We faced so much in the years of our marriage, due to lifestyle , mindset,and perception changes and believe me all of that matters.

The bible says, that what God put together let no man put asunder. So the question for you right now is: Did God put you together? If you both decide that Kingdom marriage is something that you want to do and both are committed to doing all that it takes to get there. God will get the glory.

WAR FOR YOUR MARRIAGE

I believe that God will bless your marriage and sanctify it regardless of how it started.

The bible also says that a saved wife can sanctify her husband and a saved husband can sanctify his wife. So in Christ there is always hope. For me, the fight for my marriage was an opportunity not only to fight for what I loved, but to show what unconditional love looked like. It was a chance for me to grow spiritually not only as an individual but also for us as a couple. The war for your marriage can also show you what is inside of you.

Most Marriages break down because many don't want to understand or adapt to the fact that marriage is not a ministry of me. We change physically, mentally, and emotionally. Your needs when you first get married will not be the same as time progresses. So why war for marriage? Because two are better than one. If God can forgive us for all the things we did we can surely do our best to save our covenant and vows to each other. You want to fight for the reason you decided to marry your spouse in the first place. Unless you married for the wrong reason now you need to find a reason to work it out.

WAR FOR YOUR MARRIAGE

When marriages dissolve there are casualties.They may manifest right away but at some point they can and will. Do your best to preserve the fruit of your union so that it doesn't go rotten.

If we take the time to war, listen and decipher through our breakdowns we would be able to identify the real enemy in the war instead of pointing at each other.

It's time to declare and decree over your marriage, what you want to see. You must bring down all spirits of strife and division, closing every door that the enemy may try to gain access through.

I declare Ecclesiastes 4:9-12 (NIV) over marriages. It states that two are better than one and you will have a good reward for your toil. I declare that those that have Godly marriages will stick together and not leave one another. So that when one falls the other will be there to lift the fallen one up!

I declare that we will fight the good fight of faith together in unity with the Lord for a threefold cord is not quickly broken. 1 Timothy 6:12 (NLT), Ecclesiastes 4:12 (NLT).

WAR FOR YOUR MARRIAGE

I declare Peace over my marriage not the peace that the world gives but the peace that the father gives, I will not allow my heart to be troubled or afraid.

I declare I will be on guard for my marriage, stand firm in the faith; I will be courageous and strong according to 1 Corinthians 16:13 (NLV).

I come against the adversary that prowls like a roaring lion seeking whom he may devour. 1 Peter 5:8 (NIV).

I declare Mark 10:9 (NLT) that what God has joined together, let not man separate. I declare war by holding my marriage in honor and not allowing the marriage bed to be undefiled.

I declare Psalm 85:10 (NIV) that our marriage is where steadfast love and faithfulness meet; and righteousness and peace kiss each other.

I declare 1 Peter 4:8 (NIV) that Above all,I will keep loving my spouse earnestly because love covers a multitude of sins. I declare that above all I put on love, which binds everything together in perfect harmony according to Colossians 3:14 (NIV).

WAR FOR YOUR MARRIAGE

I declare that we will abide by the new commandment that has been given to us according to John 13:34-35 (NIV) that we love one another: just as Christ has loved us. By this all people will know that we are disciples of Christ, by the love we have for another.

I declare that the love in my marriage is strong and I show the greatest love by laying down my life for my spouse according to John 15:13 (NIV).

I declare that my marriage shall have faith, hope, and love abiding in it, but the greatest of these is love 1 Corinthians 13 :13 (NKJV).

Husbands

I declare war for my marriage by living with my wife in an understanding way showing honor to her as she is the weaker vessel but she is an heir with me in the grace of life so that my prayers may not be hindered. According to 1 Peter 3:7 (ESV).

I declare that when I found my wife I found a good thing because according to Proverbs 18:22 (ASV) - He who finds a wife finds a good thing and obtains favor from Jehovah.

WAR FOR YOUR MARRIAGE

I declare that I shall hold fast to my wife and we shall become one flesh according to Ephesians 5:31(NKJV).

I declare that as a husband I will love my wife just as Christ loved the church and I will give myself up for her according to Ephesians 5:25 (NIV).

I declare that as a husband I will be completely humble and gentle, patient bearing with my wife in love, making every effort to keep the unity of the Spirit through the bond of peace according to Ephesians 4:2-3 (NIV).

I declare that over all these virtues I put on love for love shall bind us together in perfect unity according to Colossians 3:14 (NIV).

I declare that I will build up my wife and do everything in love, being kind, forgiving and compassionate according to 1 Thessalonians 5:11(NIV), 1 Corinthians 16:14 (NIV), Ephesians 4:32 (NIV).

I declare that I will be devoted to my wife in love and honor her above myself according to Romans 12:10 (NIV).

WAR FOR YOUR MARRIAGE

Wives

I declare that I will not be a quarrelsome wife according to Proverbs 21:9 (NIV).

I declare that I am a prudent wife to my husband which is a wife from the Lord according to Proverbs 19:14(NIV).

I declare that I am An excellent wife, I am the crown of my husband, I will not bring shame to him according to Proverbs 12:4 (NIV).

I declare that I am self- controlled and pure, busy at home and kind, and subject to my husband. Titus 2:5 (ESV).

I declare that I am a woman worthy of respect, I will not have malicious talk but I will be trustworthy in everything I do according to 1 Timothy 3:11 (NIV).

I declare that I am a wise woman that builds my house with my own hands and does not tear it down. Proverbs 14:1 (NIV).

I declare that I am a wife of noble character that is worth far more than rubies and pearls. Proverbs 31:10 (AMP)

WAR FOR YOUR MARRIAGE

I declare that I will be a good wife so that my husband will have full confidence in me and lack nothing of value, I will bring him good and not harm all the days of my life Proverbs 31:11-12 (NIV).

I declare that I will love my husband with an everlasting love and unfailing kindness according to Jeremiah 31:3 (NIV)

I declare mercy, and peace and my love shall always be in abundance for my husband according to Jude 1:2(NIV).

I decree that everything I do I shall do it in love.
1 Corinthians 16:14 (AMP)

I declare that I will follow my husband as he follows Christ in the example of Christ walking in faith,integrity and dedication to the Lord according to 1 Corinthians 4:16 (NIV).

CHAPTER FIVE

I DECLARE WAR FOR MY BLOODLINE

CHAPTER FIVE

I DECLARE WAR FOR MY BLOODLINE

Knowing our bloodline history tells us the essence of who we are. Have you ever wondered why you do things the way you do? Or think the way you think? Many can look in the mirror and clearly see the many physical features we possess that stem from the people who came before us.

At my grandmother's funeral I met so many new relatives that I was told I knew. Honestly, I knew names but not so much the faces or memories of the people. As I looked at many of them I started to notice how much we all resembled parts of my grandmother. The high cheek bones and the height of many of the women. The dark circles around our eyes. These were all features that repeated itself throughout our bloodline.

Your bloodline can tell you a lot about your culture, your history and where it originally started. It can also help when it comes to your physical health. Knowing ailments, afflictions, blessings and curses that may be in your family's bloodline can help you to preserve your life and the generations after you.

I DECLARE WAR FOR MY BLOODLINE

Before you read these prayers that declare war for your bloodline. I want you to make a list of anything you can see in your bloodline that may be a curse or a hindrance. That could be stopping your bloodline from being prosperous.

Ask the Holy Spirit that leads and guides you into all truth to reveal to you areas where things may be hidden and to uncover any agreements and covenants from your ancestors that need to be broken off your bloodline.

No matter how small or insignificant you may feel it is, write it down, renounce it, and uproot it. You may have to add a fast depending on what the Holy Spirit reveals to you regarding the level of power and authority that spirit or principality may have over your bloodline.

God sent his son Jesus to redeem us and reconcile us back to him along with restoring our God given power over the enemy. It's our job to enforce that power and authority when something has been found trespassing our territory.

I DECLARE WAR FOR MY BLOODLINE

I call on heaven's defense system to fight on behalf of my bloodline. I send out special forces of warring angels to go behind enemy lines and take back those that have been taken captive by the enemy.

I cancel all covenants and contracts known and unknown.

I close every door and portal that has given the kingdom of darkness access to operate in my life, my children's, and my children's children's life.

I cancel all curses down to the last generation and legacy of my bloodline. I cleanse my bloodline with the blood of Jesus for the blood still works and has power.

I declare that those that are born in the latter part of the bloodline shall do greater than the former; they shall live holy, consecrated lives, set apart for God and have the knowledge of God.

They shall be a bloodline of Glory that worships God in spirit and in truth.I disallow and break generational curses of Alcoholism, Drug addictions, mental illness and low self esteem.

I command it to cease and desist now in Jesus Name.

I DECLARE WAR FOR MY BLOODLINE

I bind up all manner of sickness and disease such as high blood pressure, cancer, heart attack and obesity, copd, and asthma. I declare that by the stripes of Jesus Christ all are healed.

I bind up and rebuke premature death; we break its hold and close off its access.

I declare that my obedience to the father makes my bloodline righteous.

I stand in the gap on their behalf. I speak long life to my bloodline.

I decree a multiplication of wealth that shall lead to generational wealth. I pray that the grace of God is sufficient for them.

I declare that I am strong in the Lord and in his mighty power. I put on the full armor of God, so that I can take my stand against the devil's schemes. 2 Corinthians 10:5 (NIV), Ephesians 6:10-11 (NIV), Peter 5:8 (NIV).

I decree that the genealogy of my bloodline shall produce mighty men and women of God.

Karen Gates

I DECLARE WAR FOR MY BLOODLINE

I pray that my bloodline shall be a line of honor and dignity to one another and God. I decree this shall be a bloodline that devotes themselves to prayer.

I declare that a string of love,hope, grace and forgiveness is weeded within my bloodline binding us together in unity.

I declare that they shall seek the Lord's prescience continually.

I decree that not one generation shall be lost to this world. Every generation shall live with the foundation of Christ.

I declare the peace of God, the purpose of God and that the Love of God shall forever burn within our hearts and that none will depart from it.

I break the strongholds of unrighteousness, iniquity, unforgiveness, and replace it with righteousness of Christ, forgiveness and holy living. in Jesus Name Amen.

CHAPTER SIX

WAR ON THE HIERARCHY OF HELL

CHAPTER SIX

WAR ON THE HIERARCHY OF HELL

The Kingdom of God has order and rank and so does the kingdom of darkness. The kingdom of darkness is a well organized kingdom that works together to bring down and do its best to overthrow the kingdom of heaven and tries to discredit what Jesus did on the cross. Their goal is to take down as many believers as they can by causing chaos, confusion and destruction that makes many lose hope and give up. They know their orders and they don't break rank trying to gain authority over each other.

A hierarchy is a system of organizing people into different ranks or levels of importance.

When you are coming against the different ranks of hell you strategically remove and bring down invisible forces that cannot be seen by the naked eye.

Ephesians 6:12 (NIV).says, we wrestle not against flesh and blood A common mistake that is made in time of war is We try to fight a spiritual battle with flesh and fist. I decree that their minds are set on things above and not of this world. Colossians 3:2 (AMP).

WAR ON THE HIERARCHY OF HELL

When we see a man or woman operating in an evil and deceptive manner we look at what we see in natural instead of asking for the revelation of who is really behind the madness. This is why it is imperative that as believers we read our word and study it daily,That we may identify these types of things that come to kill, steal and destroy.

Those that reside in the KIngdom of God have to start seeing themselves as God sees us.The spies that went to spy out the land of Canaan came back with the report that what God said was in the land was there. But they also came back with the report that there were giants in the land. Their problem was they only saw themselves as tiny little grasshoppers.

It's time to rise up and walk in the power within us knowing that the power we have can overthrow anything that is a threat to us obtaining the promise of God for our life. They knew in order to possess the land they were going to have to fight the giants.

WAR ON THE HIERARCHY OF HELL

The Kingdom of darkness understands their goal: they work in unity to destroy the works of God's great and wonderful Kingdom. They do not want heaven to reign on earth. This war is a fight but the good news is that in the end we win, because we have the mighty Ghibbor, the one who fights for us and he's never lost a battle.

I declare war on the kingdom of darkness by binding up the strongman that comes to our houses and tries to carry off our goods and possessions while plundering our house strongly. Matthew 12:29 (NIV).

I declare war on the principalities in operation in our government that passes laws that are in direct conflict with laws of God. I declare Isaiah 9:6 (NIV) that says, the government sits on God's shoulders.

I declare that we shall have Godly leaders that believe in and enforce that which is in heaven. To be made manifest in the earth.

WAR ON THE HIERARCHY OF HELL

I declare war against the powers of hell that would come up against me. For I have the power to overcome all the power of the enemy; and nothing will harm me according to Luke 10:19 (NIV).

I disband all the power that the kingdom of darkness possesses and uses to try and bring down marriages, families, government and the church.

I declare that I shall be strengthened with all power according to his glorious might so that I may have great endurance and patience in the fight. Colossians 1:11 (NIV).

I declare war against the rulers of darkness of this world.

I declare that I will use discernment to uncover those that are disguised as angels of light but are really angels of darkness.

I declare those who have had their minds and souls overtaken by demonic forces and cant see their way out. That the mind of Christ is their portion and the eyes of their understanding enlightened.

WAR ON THE HIERARCHY OF HELL

I declare Philippians 4: 7 (NIV), that the peace of God which transcends all understanding, will guard their hearts and minds in Christ Jesus.

I declare war against all spiritual wickedness in high places. I demolish arguments and every pretension that sets itself up against the truth and knowledge of God is. I take captive every thought to make it obedient to Christ. I decree that I am alert and of sober mind.

CHAPTER SEVEN

WAR ON OPPRESSION-DEPRESSION-REJECTION

Chapter Seven

WAR ON OPPRESSION -DEPRESSION- REJECTION

The King James Version dictionary defines oppression as to load or burden with unreasonable impositions; treat with unjust severity, rigor or hardship, to oppress a nation with taxes or contributions,to oppress one by forcing him to perform unreasonable service.

To overpower, overburden. The bible tells us that the children of Israel were oppressed by pharoah. How did they eventually break free from under their oppressive ruler? They cried out to God and God heard their cry and raised up Moses to go and tell the pharaoh to let his people go.

The assignment of the spirit of oppression is to attack your mind with the cares of the world to the degree that you can't properly function or make decisions.This is why it is very important that we guard our gates.The spirit of depression attacks your joy and your hope. This spirit causes feelings of guilt and worthlessness. How do you identify this spirit in operation in a person's life? Look for frequent mood changes and sadness that just seems to never go away. This spirit affects how people feel in a negative way.

WAR ON OPPRESSION -DEPRESSION- REJECTION

They often see no reason to do anything in their daily life and are tired and unmotivated to do anything about the way they feel.

The spirit of rejection operates by telling a person a lie that no one cares for them and their life has no value. When the spirit of rejection is in control of a person's life there is nothing that you can say to make them believe that you care regardless of how many times you say it you just have to show it.

A person under the control of this spirit feels like the black sheep of the family and everytime something goes wrong everyone blames them for it. They often feel that nothing they do is right.

They are always trying to do good to get a much needed pat on the back or word of affirmation from a person of authority. When their tactics don't yield the result they want They act out in aggressive and angry behavior to get attention even if it's not the intended response they were looking for. This spirit, just like all others, can be overcome and overthrown through the power of Christ.

We can pray and ask the Holy Spirit to show us the root. The origin of how these spirits came in and built a foundation.

WAR ON OPPRESSION -DEPRESSION- REJECTION

Then we must uproot it in the spirit, with prayer.There must be repentance from the person that is bound with this spirit. Through repentance there shall be restoration of the person back to the father understanding who they are in God and the power and authority that have in Christ Jesus.

I declare war against the spirit of oppression that comes to keep God's people pressed down under cruel and unjust treatment. I bind this spirit that abuses its power and authority to prevent the people of God from getting ahead.

I decree that its power is broken and all that are bound shall walk in freedom that God has freely given. I declare to Pharaoh must let the people of God go in Jesus' name.

I come against every spirit that has unjustly oppressed me or the people I love with heavy burdens that leave us with no hope of ever progressing in life or the things of God. I cancel the assignment of the oppressor(s) in my life,my family and friends lives. I decree that I am highly favored by God, I am a vessel of honor, and I am free indeed because the son has set me free .

WAR ON OPPRESSION -DEPRESSION- REJECTION

I declare war on the spirit of depression by declaring that the Joy of the Lord is my strength and this is the day that the Lord has made I will rejoice and be glad in it.

I cancel all triggers and memories that hold me in a sad state that I am not able to function in my day to day life. I bind up guilt, fatigue, mood swings, loss of appetite, thoughts of suicide and death in Jesus Name.

I can do all things through Christ that strengthens me and his Spirit is powerfully working within me according to Colossians 1:29 (NIV).

I decree that the blood of Jesus saved me and covers me. It has separated me from sin as far as the east is from the west according to Psalm 103:12 (NIV).

I declare that when I confess my sins God forgives me and purifies me according to 1 John 1:9(NIV). I believe that God has cleansed me from my guilty conscience. In Jesus name.

WAR ON OPPRESSION -DEPRESSION- REJECTION

I come against the spirit of suicide that has pierced the soul with unprocessed pain trauma. I break every covenants and agreements with the spirit of death

I decree I will live and not die and declare the works of the Lord according to Psalm 118:17(KJV) .

I shut down and silence every voice that comes to convince me that there isn't another way out and that my life is of no value and of no use.

 I bind up feelings of hopelessness, I bind up anger,rage, agitation and reckless unruly behavior.

I take the emotions that cause me to have mood swings and I place them back into God's hands who will uphold me with his righteous hand.I declare over my life peace that passes all understanding.

I clothed myself in the blanket of comfort and grace. I speak healing into my heart and mind.

I renounce every sin that I have committed and close every door that I have opened to the Kingdom of darkness. Lord, I ask that you come into my heart and into my mind, cleanse me, wash me, make me whole.

WAR ON OPPRESSION -DEPRESSION- REJECTION

I decree, I am a new creation. Old things have passed away and behold all things are new.I expel any and all darkness now In Jesus Name.

Holy Spirit, I ask you to come in and fill my temple and evict anything that is not like God. I give you permission to sweep the house clean. I declare that all things are going to work together for my good.

I declare that I will not give power to situations or words that come up in my life that's negative.

I declare war against the spirit of rejection, that imposes thoughts of feeling unloved and unwanted. I bind low self esteem, mistrust, bitterness, Overreacting,
aggressiveness, abandonment, lowliness and unforgiveness. I declare that I have a high opinion of myself and I will do above and beyond what I think.

I declare that God has a purpose and plan for me that has been in place since before he formed me in my mother's womb. I declare that I will not blow up or exaggerate or go to extremes in situations that may not be in my favor. I declare I will be peaceful and friendly to others.

WAR ON OPPRESSION -DEPRESSION- REJECTION

I declare that I will be strong and courageous for it is the Lord God who goes with me and he will never leave or forsake me according to Dueteronomy 31:6 (NLT).

I declare that I will take refuge under the shadow of God's wings whenI feel alone Psalm 36:7 (NIV).

I declare that even if my father, mother or family abandoned me that God will hold me close Psalm 27:10 (NIV).

I renounce all things that proceed from within that defile me according to Mark 7:21-23 (NIV).

I ask you God to heal my mind and my thoughts help me decipher through my emotions. Show me how to express them in a proper and constructive manner.

Lord, I forgive those who have abandoned me knowingly and unknowingly.

I declare that God loves me so much that he gave his son Jesus to die on the cross for me which brought me reconciliation and redemption.

CHAPTER EIGHT

VICTORY AGAINST THE DEVOURER

Chapter Eight

VICTORY AGAINST THE DEVOURER

Lord, I remind you of your word that you will rebuke the devourer for my sake Malachi 3: 8 (NIV). The devourer has come to try and destroy all that me and my family have worked for. I declare war against every enemy that comes to kill, steal and destroy. John 10:10 (NIV) .

I declare war against the spirit of the frugivore over my life and my families.

I close off every door of access that has been open. I shut you down and out.

I decree my faith is strong because my hope and trust is in God.

I come against the spirit of sickness, For my God heals my diseases according to Psalm 103:3 (NIV).

I declare victory over disease, the palmerworm and the cankerworm that would come to eat up my crops in Jesus Name. I declare that the stripes of Jesus Christ gave me victory and no affliction can overtake or devour me according to Isaiah 53: 5 (NKJV).

VICTORY AGAINST THE DEVOURER

I declare that my health is restored and my wounds are healed by the power of Jesus' Name.

Lord I declare that just as the lions did not devourer Daniel in the lion's den that which comes to devourer shall lie down in peace with me Psalm 4:8 (ASV).

I declare victory in my finances because I sow sparingly and reap sparingly, I also sow generously and reap generously according to 2 Corinthians 9:6 (AMP).

For you God, give me the ability to produce wealth, Deuteronomy 8:18 (AMPC),and I will not throw my pearls to swine. Matthew 7:6 (ASV).

I declare that you my God shall meet all of my needs according to the riches of your glory in Christ Jesus Philipians 4:19(NIV).

I declare that no weapon formed against me shall prosper Isaiah 54:17 (NIV)   and I will be victorious. Devil you cannot have my crops, my harvest,my family or finances.

VICTORY AGAINST THE DEVOURER

I decree that I have victory over the devourer because I seek first the Kingdom of God and all of its righteousness and everything shall be added unto me. Matthew 6:3 (NIV).

I decree that with God I have victory after victory and trample down on those that oppose me and come to devourer me.

I am more than conqueror, I overcome the devourer by the blood of the lamb and the word of my testimony according to Revelation 12:11 (KJV)

CHAPTER NINE

WAR AGAINST THE ACCUSER SPIRIT

Chapter Nine
WAR AGAINST THE ACCUSER SPIRIT

I bind up and declare war against every spirit that operates like satan who is the accuser of brethren who accuse me day and night but there is no condemnation for those who are in Christ Jesus.

I declare that all false accusations that rise up against me are silenced for this is the benefit of being a servant of the Lord according to Isaiah 54:17 (NIV).

I declare that because I am the righteous of Christ by knowledge, I am delivered according to Proverbs 11:9 (NIV).

I declare war against every enemy whose mouth does not tell the truth and in their hearts they destroy others because they use their tongues for telling lies according to Psalm 5:9 (NIV).

I declare that I will be strong and courageous. I will not be discouraged in the face of false accusations for God moves about in my camp to protect me and deliver me from my enemies according to Deuteronomy 23:14 (NIV).

WAR AGAINST THE ACCUSER SPIRIT

I decree that every lying lip that comes to accuse me be silenced for with pride and contempt they speak arrogantly against me when they know I am righteous according to Psalm 31:18(NIV).

I declare the lies and accusations of the enemy are powerless; they shall fall to the ground and yield no fruit, May every negative word be scorched and wither like the seed that fell on stony ground. I resist the devil and he will flee. James 4:7(NIV).

I decree that I will forgive those who bear false witness against me according to Exodus 20:16 (ESV).

I come against lies, slander and accusations. I declare that surely goodness, mercy and truth with unfailing love will pursue me all the days of my life. Nothing by any means would be able to hurt me.

I put away anger, wrath, malice,slander, and obscene talk from my mouth. Colossians 3:7-8 (ESV).

I declare that I am blessed when people falsely say all kinds of evil against me. I will rejoice and be glad for great is my reward in heaven Matthew 5:11-12 (ESV).

WAR AGAINST THE ACCUSER SPIRIT

I declare that like Jesus when He was oppressed, and afflicted he opened not his mouth he was brought like a lamb led to the slaughter according to Isaiah 53:7 (KJV).

I declare that no harsh words shall come out of my mouth because what comes out the mouth proceeds from the heart and this is what defiles a person and I shall not be defiled. Matthew 15 :18 (ESV)

Lord, I ask that you create in me a clean heart and renew a right spirit within me according to Psalm 51:10 (ESV). I declare that I forgive them for they know not what they do.Luke 23:34 (ESV).

I cleanse my heart and get rid of all bitterness, rage and anger, brawling and slander, along with every form of malice and unforgiveness that I may be harboring in my heart according to Esphesians 4:31 (NIV.Father just as you have forgiven me and shown me love and grace I will do unto others as you have done for me..

I will not allow anything to block me from your divine love and glory. I will walk in favor and blessings for all my days in Jesus Name Amen.

CHAPTER TEN

I'M RECOVERING ALL

Chapter Ten

I'M RECOVERING ALL

I declare that everything the enemy has stolen I have recovered all and now I declare to him who is able to do exceedingly and abundantly above all that I could ask, or think according to the power that works within me be Glorified for the things he has done. Ephesians 3:20   (NKJV) , Romans 11:36 (NLT).

I receive double for my trouble. I decree my peace and my joy is restored, my love is restored, my faith is restored, my trust is restored, and my finances are restored In Jesus Name.

I declare that When the spirit of the Lord comes upon me It gives me the power to go into the enemy camp and take back what he stole from me. It gives me the power to trample over serpents and scorpions and all the power of the enemy and nothing shall by any means will hurt me.

.

I'M RECOVERING ALL

I know he will restore me,and bring me up from the midst of the trouble.

I thank you for increasing my honor and comforting me. Psalm 71:20-21 (NIV).

I cast my cares on you for you will sustain me and never let me be shaken according to (Psalm 55:22 NIV).

I decree my family shall recover from every loss, every heartache, every affliction.

I decree I will wait upon the Lord, I will run and not get weary of doing well.

For my strength is renewed like the eagle because my hope is in the Lord and I will not faint Isaiah 40:31 (NIV).

I declare everywhere I look restoration and blessings Amos 9:13 (NIV). I decree restoration of the years that swarming locust has eaten Joel 2:25 (NIV).

I declare restoration of my soul for God restores my soul and leads me in paths of righteousness for his name sake. Psalm 23:3 (NIV).

I'M RECOVERING ALL

I decree that because I have restoration and recovery that what God has planned for me since the beginning of the foundations of the earth shall come to pass in my life for his word cannot return void. Isaiah 55:11 (NKJV)

I decree that I shall recover all so fast that my head will swim and It will happen one on the heels of another and I won't be able to keep up. Amos: 9:13 (MSG)

I declare restoration of Kingdom relationships that have been destroyed by the schemes of the enemy.

I decree recovery makes all things new for I am a new creation 2 Corinthians 5:17 (ESV).

I decree I am free In Jesus Name. I seek the Lord and I will lack no good thing. Psalm 34:10 (NIV).

I declare that the things the enemy meant for evil God has turned around for my good and it has allowed me to recover double for my trouble. Deuteronomy 30:3 (NIV)

I'M RECOVERING ALL

I declare this is my recovery season, my due season. This is the season that the locust,the palmerworm and cankerworm are devoured.

The season that I am the head and not the tail, the season I am above and not beneath. The season I shall lack nothing. I declare supernatural abundance above all I could ask or even think.

I declare that I have recovered all because God is not a man that he should lie nor the son of man that he should repent in Jesus Name.

Thank you Lord for being with me and being my mighty Ghibbor the Lord mighty in battle. I thank the Lord that although I may see trouble you will never leave me nor forsake me for you stick closer than brother and are a faithful friend.

CHAPTER ELEVEN

PRAYERS OF SALVATION-PEACE-BLESSINGS

Chapter Eleven

PRAYERS OF SALVATION -PEACE- BLESSINGS

Salvation

Lord, I come humbly to you. For I am a sinner and I'm asking you to forgive me. I believe that you died on the cross for my sins and rose from the dead. I repent, and ask you to come into my heart and my life. I trust you. I believe you. I accept you as my Lord and Savoir In Jesus Name Amen. If you have repeated this prayer, welcome the family of God. Next step: find a church home where you can be taught the word of God and be discipled in your new way of living.

Peace

Lord, I ask for your peace, the peace that passes all understanding. I ask for peace in my body, soul and spirit. I come against all demonic activity that causes distractions that disrupt my peace. I give no place to stress, grief or sorrow. I activate joy, peace and love in my life. Let the peace of God surround me. I strive to be at peace with all men. I ask that you keep me in perfect peace. Lord, I ask that you bless me with grace, love, peace, prosperity and strength in times of trouble. When I feel weak you are strong. Take my heart of stone and give me a heart of flesh.

PRAYERS OF SALVATION -PEACE- BLESSINGS

Blessings

I pray that the Lord makes me rich and adds no sorrow. I ask Lord that you keep smiling and being gracious to me, look my way and give me blessings

that are thirty, sixty and one hundred fold. I declare that my blessings will overtake me; they shall be pressed down, shaken together and that they run over. Lord, I pray generational blessings over my family even until my bloodline until it
reaches its end. Lord bless me indeed and cover my family In Jesus Name.

Additional Books By Karen Gates

The Power Of A Voice

Power Of A Voice Activation Prayers

Discovering The Power of Your Voice Workbook

Karen Gates

Mastering Your Voice Workbook

Discovering the Power Of Your Voice(**A compilation book of testimonies)**

Becoming: The Transformation

Becoming The Transformation Workbook

The Power of A Jezebel Spirit The Ugly Truth

Uncovering the Face Of An Enemy(Spiritual warfare Training Manual)

Build Me an Altar (Altar Team Training)

The Power Of Prayer Volume 1- The Making Of An Intercessor

The Power Of Prayer Volume 2- Intercessor Arise

The Power Of Prayer Workbook Intercessors Arise

Damaged The Power Of A Drop

I Decree Rapid Rapid Rapid Over Your Life: You Will Have What You Say

Are You Good Enough?

The Power To Declare War

The Frugivore: The Fight For Your Fruit

The Power To Jump

Biblical References & Definitions

Unless otherwise stated all bible quotes have been taken from the:

New International Version (NIV)
New Living Translation(NLV)
New King James Version(NKJV)
King James Version(KJV)
New English Standard Version (NESV)
Christian Standard Bible (CSB),
New American Standard Bible(NASB),
New English Translation(NET)
Revised Standard Version(RSV)
American Standard Version(ASV)
King James Version Dictionary

https://www.merriam-webster.com/,

http://www.google.com

http://www.biblegateway.com

http://wwweaglefamily.org

Chapter 1 -Nehemiah 4

Chapter 2 - Isaiah 54:17, 2 Thessalonians 3:3, Psalm 46:1, Psalm 133:1, Isaiah 41:10, Psalm 121:8, Colossians 3:13, 1 Corinthians 13:47, Exodus 14:4, 1 Peter 4:8, Ephesians 4:29, Proverbs 22:6, Hebrews 10:24-25.

Chapter 3- N/A

Chapter 4 - Hebrews 13:4, Ecclesiastes 4:9-12, John 14:27, 1 Corinthians 16:3, 1 Peter 5:8,Mark 10:9, Psalm 85: 10, 1 Peter 4:8, Colossians 3:14, John 13: 34-35, John 15:13, 1 Corinthians 13:13, 1 Corinthians 16:14, Proverbs 18 :22, Ephesians 5:31, 1 Peter 3:7,Proverbs 31:11-12, Proverbs 21:9, Proverbs 19:4, Proverbs 12 :4, Titus 2:5, 1 Timothy 3:11, Proverbs 44:1, Proverbs 31:10

Chapter 5- Haggai 2:9, 1 John 1:7-9, John 4:24, Romans 6:16-18, 2 Corinthians 12:9, Psalm 24:6

Chapter 6 -Ephesians 6:12, Matthew 12:29, Isaiah 9:6, Luke 10:19, Colossians 1:11, Philippians 4:7, Colossians 3:2, 2 Corinthians 10:5, Ephesians 6:10-11, 1 Peter 5:8

Chapter 7 - Philippians 4:13, Colossians 1:29, Psalm 103:12, 1 John 1:9, Deuteronomy 31:6, Psalm 36:7, Psalm 27:10, Mark 7: 21-23

Chapter 8 - Malachi 3:11, John 10:10, Isaiah 54:17, Psalm 103:3, Isaiah 53:5, Psalm 4:8, 2 Corinthians 9:6,

Deuteronomy 8:18, Matthew 7:6, Philippians 4:19, Matthew 6:33,1 Corinthians 5:7, 1 John 5:4

Chapter 9 - Isaiah 54:17, Proverbs 11:9, Psalm 5:9, Deuteronomy 23:14, Psalm 31:18, James 4:7, Exodus 20:16, Matthew 5:11-12, Colossians 3:7-8, Matthew 15:18, Psalm 51:10, Luke 23:24

Chapter 10 - Psalm 71:20-21, Psalm 55:22, Isaiah 40:31, Psalm 34:10, Amos 9:13, Joel 2:25, Psalm 23:3

The Power To Declare War

Povministries.wordpress.com
To contact the Author for speaking engagements :
povministries@gmail.com

Karen Gates

The Power To Declare War

Made in the USA
Las Vegas, NV
08 August 2024